Stay Grounded

MELINDA R. CORDELL

Stay Grounded

Soil Building for Sustainable Gardens

Easy-Growing Gardening Guide Vol. 9

Melinda R. Cordell

Rosefiend Publishing.

For more information, contact the publisher at rosefiend@gmail.com.

ISBN: 978-1-57067-395-5

For more information (and books!), visit www.melindacordell.com

Subscribe to my Newsletter and get a free gardening book: https://melindacordell.com/subscribe/

CONTENTS

"A little land well tilled,
A little house well filled,
A little wife well willed,
Are great riches."

Most of that is good, but anybody who calls me a "well-willed
little wife" is going to get a boot in his butt.

THE SOIL FOOD WEB

To see the world in a grain of sand
And a heaven in a wild flower

SOIL IS FASCINATING. THE SOIL'S ecosystem is teeming with worms, ants, bacteria (many of which are good -- even the bacteria on your hands), protozoa, springtails, miles and miles of fungi, moles and voles -- the list goes on and on. All of these creatures enrich the soil in many different ways.

Worms are a good indicator of how alive your soil is. If you don't see many worms when you dig, your soil may need help. If you see a lot of worms when you're digging, then you have a healthy soil biomass. More about this in the earthworm chapter.

3

Contrary to popular belif, plants take an active role in ordering their environment. Plants actually have ways to encourage the life of the soil to take up residence around them by secreting many different kinds of compounds into the soil through their roots. These secretions are called root exudates. As early as 1904, scientists noticed that microbes are more abundant in this zone around the roots. Root exudates contain carbohydrates (which include sugar), enzymes, amino acids, and a number of carbon-based compounds, which include valuable proteins.

Soil organisms, attracted by this deliciousness, flock over to load up at this root buffet, and take up residence in a thin zone right up against the roots – the rhizosphere – so they can chow down.

Bacteria and fungi consume the exudates. Larger microbes, such as nematodes and protozoas, come in and eat the smaller microorganisms. All these creatures excrete wastes, which the plant roots are very happy to absorb as nutrients.

Those protozoa and nematodes, in turn, are eaten by arthropods, which are eaten by other insects, birds, and animals.

What's more, the plant can control the numbers and types of fungi and bacteria they attract by changing the types of exudates they produce, depending on what the plant needs during that particular season.

But there's more.

Let's slide the scale back to the microscopic and look

at soil bacteria, those single-celled organisms. Bacteria are so tiny, that they need to cling to things in order to survive. So, bacteria produce a thin film called a biofilm that sticks to things (and sticks the bacteria to things). If you've ever seen the nasty slime inside a garbage disposal, that's biofilm to the max. In the soil, the biofilm is just thick enough to allow the bacteria to stick to soil particles, and, as an additional side effect, it also causes individual soil particles to stick to other particles. Fungal hyphae, the threads that make up fungus underground, also assists in this microscopic binding of particles. (Fun fact: Fungus actually lives underground. Mushroom are actually their fruiting bodies – their version of flowers and fruit. If plants lived this way, all the stems and leaves would be under ground, and their flowers, fruits, and seeds would be above ground.)

The soil clumps that develop, all with the help of bacteria, fungi, and other creatures, are called soil aggregates, and when you have a lot of healthy aggregates, you get great soil structure.

When you compare bare soil to the soil that's around plant roots, you'll find a far higher number of microbes – an underground community – around plant roots.

Earthworms, digging animals, insects, and other small creatures burrow through the soil, creating burrows and gaps that allow air and water to percolate through the soil. Living creatures of all sizes and kinds makes good soil health possible.

Soil Critters Also Add Nutrients

Of course, when a soil-dwelling creature dies, it passes on nutrients to other creatures to be absorbed by fungi, or eaten by bacteria. Bug poop and worm castings are also broken down, releasing more nutrients into the soil for plants to absorb.

What's more, this organic system holds nutrients in the soil where the roots are, and the nutrients aren't washed away, but become a valuable part of the soil. When the plants themselves die, they are also consumed and decayed – but the nutrients they release into the soil also stay in place for other creatures and plants to consume. Pretty slick!

On the other hand, chemical fertilizers have no staying power in the root zone. That which isn't absorbed quickly by the roots keeps draining through the soil, carried by the water, until it reaches the water table far below, where it is simply wasted – and, technically, adds a little more pollution to the water.

Control Disease Through the Soil Food Web!

Naturally, as in any world, you're going to have your good guys and bad guys and opportunists. For lo, there are plenty of pathogenic bacteria and fungi doing their part to make your plants sick.

On the other hand, the good, beneficial, and indifferent creatures tend to outweigh the troublemakers. If you have a healthy diversity of creatures and species in one area, there will always be some predator around to eat up the troublemakers and keep their numbers down. This diversity of creatures can also keep the troublemakers down by existing in such numbers that the troublemakers can't get enough food, shelter, and are outcompeted to death in a very Darwinic way.

Diversity also benefits plants. Fungi forms nets around the roots, called mycorrhiza, protecting plants from invasion from unfriendly species. Mycorrhiza sets up a partnership with plant roots that replaces the root hairs, and absorbs water and soil nutrients, which are transmitted to the roots. When the right microscopic fungi exist in the soil, this symbiotic partnership can exist.

Furthermore, when good bacteria create a thin, slimy biofilm on surfaces, pathogenic bacteria can't get a foothold on those areas, but slide on past. There are any number of defenses that a healthy, diverse ecosystem throws up against attackers. But when these defenses are taken away, the plants are susceptible to attack from unfriendly species.

That's why it's so important to have diversity in the soil (as well as above the soil and in life in general) where different species develop many complex partnerships to improve life overall. If you have a prosperous, healthy food web teeming with many different forms of life, it's very difficult for one species to take over and cause an infestation.

How Chemical Fertilizers Affect the Soil Biomass

I know an older lady who had a nice little flower bed out front of her apartment, and she'd occasionally have me weed it and hoe it a little to help her out. The soil was surprisingly hard; I had to chop it with the hoe, and the resulting till consisted of rough chunks and powder. There were no pores or air spaces in the soil because there were no worms. The reason? For years she fed the plants with granular fertilizer – not compost.

Why would using granular fertilizer reduce soil to such a state? Because when plants are fed with chemicals, the plants stop using the microbial network that is at their fingertips – or root-tips – below the soil. That network is a "use it or lose it" kind of setup.

So when the plants start relying on chemical fertilizers, they don't need to lure in microorganisms, so they stop excreting exudates. As a result, the tiny organisms that had been congregating around the roots drift away, and the effect is felt all the way up the food chain.

Also, chemical fertilizers themselves affect the creatures in the soil. Worms will burrow away from the synthetic nitrates in the fertilizer – a loss that is certainly felt in the soil. Without worms and the helpful creatures that live under the earth, soil loses its ability to circulate air and absorb water. The soil particles lose those little bits of bacteria biofilm, and after a while, the soil structure deteriorates. When this happens, gardening starts to take a lot more work.

This is why it's important to feed the soil naturally, with compost and mulch and other good things. It's okay to throw your plants a little chemical fertilizer if you're going to have some fancy folks over for dinner later in the week. But at the same time, your soil is better served by some organic fertilizer. It's slow-acting but the results are long-lasting, and you have the satisfaction of creating a busy world under the soil's surface.

TAKING SOIL SAMPLES

SOIL TESTING IS ONE OF the best things a gardener or farmer can do for their plants and crops. After all, a gardener can't look at the soil and say, "Whoa, we have a problem with low potassium here." And malnourished plants can't pull up their roots and move to a more fertile patch. This is why testing the soil every three to five years is so important. The test results give insight into the soil's needs and gives you ways to amend the soil to raise healthier plants and crops. You can apply the right type of fertilizer or organic material to bring the soil back into balance, and you'd use only as much fertilizer as the soil needs. This saves time and money and is environmentally sound, too.

A soil sample can be taken any time, but fall is best. Soil amended in fall has all winter to adjust, and it's ready to go just in time for spring planting.

Get Ready to Sample

As a side note, some of this chapter applies to the United States only, as I'm not sure how soil testing is done in other nations. A few years ago I did a presentation on roses to a visiting delegation from China, and was amazed to find out that they had to pay hundreds of dollars for soil testing over there. Here in the U.S., we have the University Extension, a service where many services related to homemaking, gardening, small businesses, and farming, are relatively easy and inexpensive – and these includes soil tests.

The Extension service is cost-effective, and Extension agents will have an extensive knowledge of local soils and the best ways to amend them. A private soil lab can also test your soil – just be sure it's not affiliated with a fertilizer company, as they might be in it to sell you something! Private labs can be pricier but can test your soil for additional features upon request. Some even send a representative to do your testing for you.

To start, drop by the local University Extension to pick up a box or bag for the soil sample. On the side of your sample bag or box, write the appropriate information with ballpoint pen or waterproof ink. (Do this before you take your samples, because it's hard to write on the box once the soil's inside.)

Have a clean trowel, shovel, or auger that's chrome-plated or made of stainless steel. Rusty shovels or galvanized tools will skew results. Get a clean plastic bucket to collect and mix the soil in. Finally, check the ground for moisture – the soil you're testing should crumble in the hand and not be wet.

How To Sample Your Soil

Take one sample for each specific use area – one for the garden, a separate one for the pasture, yet another one for the orchard, and so forth. If your yard has a healthy area and a sickly-looking area, sample both separately.

Within each area, take subsamples from six to eight different locations, spaced some distance apart for best results. In larger areas, such as pastures or acreage, take 10 to 15 subsamples.

Set the shovel into the soil -- about 5 to 7 inches -- and throw aside the first shovelful. Then, at the back of the hole (where the shovel's back rested), use the shovel to cut a slice about an inch thick and 5 to 7 inches deep. Pull off the thin layer of grass and roots at the top, then place the soil in the bucket. Then zigzag around the sample area as you take subsamples.

Stay about 300 feet away from gravel roads when taking samples, or the soil test will come up alkaline due to all that limestone dust. In gardens, don't take samples where beans, peas, or legumes have grown recently – these plants fix nitrogen in the soil, which also skews results. (However, farmers sampling alfalfa or soybean fields can mention this to the soil lab, and the lab will adjust the results accordingly.)

Once you've finished taking subsamples, mix them all together in the bucket, breaking big clods into crumbs. Then fill the box and mail or deliver it to the soil lab. Include the processing fee. Results return in two or three weeks, or later during busy seasons.

Filling the little box with a sample of garden soil.

Interpreting the Results

The soil report will reveal several things: the amount of

organic material in your sample soil; the amounts of phosphorus, potassium, calcium, and magnesium available to your plants; soil pH; cation exchange capacity; and fertilizer recommendations and suggestions.

Nutrients such as phosphorus, potassium, calcium, and magnesium are listed from being "very low" to "very high." Those that are listed as "low" are nutrients that your soil is especially deficient in. These levels might take a year or more to bring back to normal. Nutrient levels listed as "medium" are adequate, but it wouldn't hurt to add a little more. A "high" amount of a nutrient needs no amending. A "very high" amount should not be amended; otherwise, that nutrient may reach levels that are toxic to the plant. More is not always better!

The **pH** level of the soil shows whether the soil is acid (below 6.0), normal (6.0 to 7.0), or alkaline (8.0 to 12.0). In excessively acidic or alkaline soil, nutrients are locked away and plants can't absorb them. Lime is used to neutralize an acidic soil, which unlocks specific nutrients from the soil, which the plant's roots are then able to absorb. Adding lime is also recommended if the soil needs phosphorus, calcium, or magnesium (the last of which is available in dolomitic limestone).

Organic material (OM) is the plant or animals residue in the soil. Organic materials provides nitrogen, nutrients, and trace minerals; it helps the soil retain nutrients; and improves soil structure and water retention. A soil high in organic material can have an active biomass, which benefits soil health greatly. These benefits do not show up on soil tests. Well, a soil test can't do *everything*.

Cation (pronounced "cat-ion") **exchange capacity**, or CEC, indicates your soil's capacity to hold nutrients. A higher number often indicates a more fertile soil. Levels above 20 or 25 mean that the soil has more nutrients than plants can use in a year, while levels below 10 mean that nutrients will be depleted very quickly and will need amending. Clay soils often have a higher CEC because the microscopic, negatively-charged clay particles hold on to positively charged ions of calcium, magnesium, potassium, and nitrogen and keeps them from leaching away. Soils high in organic matter also have a higher CEC.

The soil report will also list **recommendations** on how much fertilizer to apply for different cropping options; how much lime to apply, if any; and how much nitrogen to add and when to add it.

Acting On the Results

When you start amending your soil, use organic materials for good, long-term results. Remember, soil is complex and can take a while to change, but you can coax it along. When adding lime, for instance, expect to see complete results a year after putting the lime down. This is why it's a good idea to be patient, and to pile on the compost while you're being patient!

Building a good soil won't take place overnight. Soil building is an ongoing process. Working with the soil means creating the most nourishing and healthy home for your plants to thrive in – allowing you to get the best yields from healthy crops.

EARTHWORMS: THE SUPER SOIL SAVERS

EARTHWORMS ARE A GODSEND TO the soil in your garden and yard. Having thousands of earthworms in your soil is like having a thousand tiny tillers running day and night ... and each tiller is pulling a compost spreader behind it.

That's because earthworms mix the soil as they eat their way through, and their tunnels loosen compacted clay or silt, allowing water to seep through. These tunnels also increase the aeration of the soil, sometimes up to 60 or 75%, which in turn helps the microorganisms around your plant roots to thrive. What's more, the earthworms will do this work for you all day and even while you sleep. What's not to like?

Earthworms eat soil 1) to get the organic material in it, and 2) to use bits of sand and rocks to grind up the food in their crop.

Earthworm castings (i.e. earthworm poop) are pure gold to a plant. Here's why: Worms, as they eat their way through the ground, devour organic material and soil, which are ground into extremely fine particles in the worm's crop and stomachs. This soil soup in the worm's gut is mixed with beneficial microorganisms from inside the worm, as well as the calcium from the worm's calcium gland, before it's excreted right next to the plant roots. When ordinarily-unavailable nutrients pass through a worm, the nutrients come out in chelated forms – forms that are super-easy for plant roots to absorb.

USDA tests show us that worm castings, when compared to the soil from which they were made, have about 5 times the available nitrogen, 7 times the phosphorus, 3 times the magnesium, 11 times the potassium, and 1½ times the calcium. Even the slime on the earthworm is high in nitrogen. That nitrogen is why, when you dig up a plant, you can see how the roots wrap around the sides of the earthworm burrows. Earthworm burrows also catch fertilizer runoff and bind it into the soil, trapping it and keeping it within the reach of plant roots.

Worms can produce up to *700 pounds* of castings per

acre. Imagine how much 700 pounds of fertilizer would cost! And what's more, high populations of worms – half a million worms per acre – can create about 250 miles of tunnels every week, according to the late Dennis Linden, Agricultural Research Service scientist and soil physicist. This allows heavy rains to drain into the soil and keeps the soil from getting waterlogged.

So if the worms in your soil are healthy, then you know that the soil biomass is healthy, too, and this in turn keeps your plants strong and vigorous.

Here's how to encourage those worms in your garden without a lot of heartache and hassle.

Earthworms need organic material – compost, rotted manure, decaying plants – to eat. This is essential. And once the earthworm population has increased, you'll need to keep adding organic materials to keep them fed. Cow manure, grass clippings, and green clover leaves – all high-nitrogen materials – are great for worms.

Worms also eat your kitchen waste if you spade it into the soil for them. Coffee grounds, tea bags, fruit and vegetable bits are tasty worm snacks. Worms really like meat, but you will have to watch out for animals that like it also.

The kinds of organic matter you can add are endless. For instance, worms love kitchen waste. Their favorites are lettuce and cabbage. They also like fish bones, fruit and vegetable peels, and leftovers.

A sprinkling of corn meal over the ground at night will encourage the worms to reproduce. The worms are like, "Yum, cornmeal, my favorite!" and they come up to eat, and while they're on the surface, they bump into another cute worm, also eating cornmeal. Then the magic happens.

Dig up some soil and sort through it to see how your earthworm population is doing. Look for tunnels with slick-looking walls – these are probably from nightcrawlers. It's good to have a lot of worms in your sample, but it's also good to have several different species of worms, too.

According to Dr. Linden, earthworms are creatures of habit. If they find food someplace once, they'll keep returning to get some more. If you till your organic matter in the soil, the field worms will dig along horizontally to get the food. However, if you leave your organic matter on top of the soil, the worms will dig up. These upward-facing tunnels will bring more rain and air into the soil than the horizontal burrows.

Avoid an acidic mulch, like large quantities of oak leaves or pine needles. An acid soil, one with a pH of 5.4 or less, will kill worms. If you have an acidic soil, keep mixing lime into the soil to bring the pH up, and test the soil annually to be sure it stays neutral. (However, if you are trying to grow acid-loving plants, such as blueberries, magnolias, azaleas, etc., don't lime the soil. Acid-loving plants will make their own arrangements with the soil – and they still love compost and organic materials.)

Sandy soils generally have fewer worms than silt or clay soils do. Applying more organic material will fix this, though the process will take a while.

Worms die in the summer heat or during sudden autumn freezes if they're not protected. Here is where a thick, organic mulch comes in handy. A thick mulch will keep the soil cool in summer and warm in the winter, hold moisture in the ground during the hot summer, keep weeds down, and will rot away in winter, adding nutrients to the soil. Keep adding mulch to the ground as the mulch decays.

I talk about mulch quite often in all my books. I'm on the page, hollering about mulch, and if you're not careful I'm going to show up on your street with a skid loader full of mulch, shouting "I THINK YOU SHOULD USE THIS." And you should! One of my readers in Wales was like, "Why does she talk about mulch all the time?" Then she mulched her roses, and they perked up and started growing like crazy. Now she is sold on mulch. Smart gal! You-all need to be like her.

In summer, mulch keeps the worms alive and active. When soil temperatures rise and the soil dries out, field worms will dig deep into the soil, curl up into a little ball to save water, and go dormant for a while. This is not helpful for your soil's health. However, if you put mulch on your garden, the soil will stay cool and moist, and field worms will keep digging among your plant roots. Mulch will encourage nightcrawlers to dig burrows to the surface to eat, allowing better water drainage in the ground.

One final way to protect your worm population is by

not tilling, or tilling less.

Have several areas in your garden that don't get tilled – an easy task if you have a strawberry or asparagus bed in the garden. Or have a no-till garden. Tilling through the year tears up worm burrows and kills field worms. Also, due to the highly increased aeration, organic material is broken down so much faster than in untilled soils.

Be sure to protect earthworms from hungry chickens, too.

If you prefer tilling, fall tilling is best. Tilling brings air into the soil, which insulates the earthworms against winter's extreme temperatures. Also, there are lots of young worms in the fall, so any extra organic material put underground would be good for them. After tilling, mulch the soil heavily with chopped-up leaves. The worms will remain active through the winter under the mulch, and you'll find worm castings under the leaves even in February. How's that for service?

Sometimes you'll have a soil that has been completely wrecked. Some people have subdivision soil, which is that churned-up clay left over from house construction; some people have fragipan; some have desert asphalt. If your soil is completely dead with no worms, build a raised bed on a thick layer of newspapers, adding worms and compost and organic material. You will eventually bring the soil back to life, but this process will take about 3-5 years. You will have to keep adding and keep adding the good stuff, but the microbiota and worms will return.

You can even "seed" your garden with earthworms. Find a pasture that's rich with worms, cut out a large block of soil, and plant it into your soil, digging organic material into the area all around the transplanted block. Keep laying down mulch and digging organic material into your dead soil. You can also pick up earthworms after a rain and put them in your garden, or buy them at a bait shop. (Avoid red wigglers, which live in compost only. Get nightcrawlers instead.)

Charles Darwin, who was fascinated by earthworms and wrote a whole book about them, said, "It may be doubted whether there are many other creatures which have played so important a part in the history of the world." He has an excellent point. The worms have made the soil of many nations fertile; they will do the same for your soil.

WORMS!!

HOW TO PROTECT
EARTHWORMS

THE BEST WAY IS TO UNDERSTAND the life cycle of earthworms, and then do your gardening work around that cycle, to protect the worms as much as possible. They're mature by late spring, lay eggs in summer (when worm activity declines), and in fall, new worms grow.

One very good way to help them is to mulch in the fall. I've found that 26 bags of leaves, when spread over a 16 x 25 foot space and mowed with a mulching mower, will turn into a layer of nice, shredded mulch about two inches deep. (It looks nice, too.) I didn't till it into the soil, but let it lay. In February, I peeked underneath and found tons of earthworm castings. Solid gold! Worms croak in winter if there's no mulch on ground, but they work happily in the upper soil if the soil has been mulched.

If you keep soil moist and mulched in summer, worms will stay active instead of going dormant. (This also helps your plants – and helps you keep the weeds away.) Cardboard and newspaper mulches are good.

Dig used fish or discarded produce right into the ground to give the earthworms a treat. (This doesn't work well in sandy soils, though – sometimes buried produce is simply preserved in sandy soils, instead of breaking down.)

Another way to protect earthworms, and in fact, the whole soil biomass, is to skip tilling altogether. Tilling brings air into the soil, which kicks the microbiota into overdrive, and they quickly devour the organic material in the soil before your plants have a chance to get to it. Tilling also tears up the earthworm population – if you're a field worm, scooching between soil particles, eating the dirt that's in your way, you're not going to be getting out of the tiller's way in time. (The nightcrawlers are the only worms that use a series of semi-permanent burrows – the other guys just eat their way along.)

If you must till, do it in the fall, because the same air that causes the microbiota to eat your organic material will also help insulate the earthworms against winter's freezes. Also, the worms will have a season to recover from the tilling. Fall is when their eggs hatch and the new worms grow, so any extra organic material put underground would be good for the worms.

Or, you could also have till-free zones – this is easy if you have permanent crops like asparagus or strawberries – so the worm population can make a comeback more quickly. Or plant your garden walkways in clover (which would add nitrogen to the soil) and edge them in the fall. (There will be more on the tilling/no tilling debate in a later chapter.)

Add some lime to the soil to encourage the earthworms and keep the pH close to neutral.

However, keeping a permanent mulch on the ground is best. In spring, push the mulch aside, hoe your seedbeds (or use one of those mini-tillers if hoeing is hard on your body) and put the plants in. Then replace the mulch when the plants have put on several permanent leaves, or when they're tall and husky enough. Not only will the mulch make your worms happy, but it also saves water, keeps the soil from splashing up on the leaves, keeps the soil moist, and keeps the weeds down so you're not hoeing all the livelong day.

Bring in extra worms. After the first spring rainfall, worms come up out of the ground and crawl over curbs and onto streets, where they get stuck. One year when I noticed worms everywhere on the street, I went to the local playground and found tons of them dying on the pavement. But there was a lot of leaf and grass litter against the curb, and each clump held a bunch of worms. I filled two big cups part of the way up with worms, brought them home, and put them in my garden, covering them with mulch. When I peeked at the worms an hour later, they had all burrowed away, even the one that I had not expected to survive.

If you go picking up worms, use picnic forks so your hands don't get covered with a layer of slime.

Sandy soil will naturally have fewer worms than silt or clay soils do. Worms need both organic material and mineral soil for food. Food high in nitrogen is good – the worm converts this into protein, which is rare in soil and is something they need. By adding organic material, you raise the soil's carrying capacity as well as worm population.

Chemicals, whether they're fertilizers or herbicides, can have a detrimental effect on soil dwellers. A study done by the Department of Agriculture shows that after applying ammonium sulfate to the soil for three years, earthworms were completely eliminated from the soil. Definitely not what we are after here.

A FIELD GUIDE TO EARTHWORMS

In the United States, you can find three common worms, all of which are native to Europe, each occupying different niches in the soil.

Epigeic Earthworms

These live near the soil's surface, or in the leaf litter, and munch on leaves.

Red wrigglers getting the hell out of a too-wet compost bin.
Photo by Toby Hudson

Red wrigglers *(Eisenia fetida)*

Also called tiger worms due to their stripes, or manure worms. These worms are surface dwellers only, living their little worm lives in the dead leaves and grasses on top of the soil. They are great for vermicomposting, or you can get a bunch of them to break down your cool compost pile. A smaller worm than *E. hortensis* (below).

Eisenia hortensis, aka European earthworm. Picture by Trevor Reid.

European earthworms (*Eisenia hortensis,* formerly *Dendrobaena veneta*)

These live in the leaf litter on the top of the soil, feeding on the bacteria and fungi living on the decaying leaves and pine needles. European earthworms (sometimes called nightcrawlers even though they are not) generally are found in northern forests, and are sometimes used in vermicomposting. These are larger and huskier than *E. fetida*, the red wrigglers.

Endogeic Earthworms

These live in the soil, burrowing horizontally among plant roots and munching on fungi, microorganisms, and fine root tips. They live their lives underground, rarely coming to the surface.

Dendrodrilus rubidus (the big dude) and Lumbricus rubellus (the little guy).
Photo by Donald Holbern.

Leaf worms (*Lumbricus rubellus*)

These live in the leaf layer on top of the ground as well as in the first few inches of soil. It doesn't form permanent burrows the way its big cousin, the nightcrawler, does.

Angle worms (*Aporrectodea spp.*)

Angle worms (or gray worms) are common in fields and gardens, and do a great job of mixing and improving the upper part of the soil and increasing soil permeability. If you want a nice thick layer of black soil in your garden, better get these guys.

Field worms (assorted spp.)

Field worms are most common in humid areas. They are smaller than nightcrawlers and not as vigorous, and generally live in the top six inches of the soil among the roots of your plants. They don't build semi-permanent burrows like the nightcrawlers do, but eat and push their way between soil particles. They don't eat healthy plant roots, contrary to popular belief, but they will eat rotting roots. Field worms don't put their castings on the surface as nightcrawlers do, but leave castings in the burrows behind them as they dig.

There is another field worm that is sometimes a greenish color, and when you dig him up, he's curled up in a little coil. He's a slacker.

There is also a little skinny worm that you'll find in infertile areas, and he doesn't do a whole lot, either.

Anecic Earthworms

These live deepest in the soil, making permanent vertical burrows from the depths to the surface. They're good at bringing subsoil minerals to the top where plant roots can reach them.

Nightcrawler. Photo by Rob Hille.

Nightcrawlers (*Lumbricus terrestris*)

Nightcrawlers the big muscular guys, are the gigantic worms with a dark rose/brown head and pinkish tail. They dig burrows deep into the subsoil and are surface feeders, unlike other worms that get their food as they burrow through the soil. They will peek out of the ground and grab a leaf to eat and pull it down into the burrow so they can eat their leaf in peace, and also keep the rain out.

Their burrows can travel down to six feet into the subsoil, but nightcrawlers feed and mate on the soil surface, so they're more commonly seen than other earthworms. They need lots of high-nitrogen organic matter to eat.

DON'T LET LEAVES GO TO WASTE

AND NOW THE LEAVES, STRICKEN BY that last hard frost, are drifting, even cascading, out of the trees. The wealth of the late golden maples has been flung far and wide, and the ground is golden.

Which leaves you (no pun intended) standing out in the yard, rake in hand, wondering how many weeks of hard labor this cleanup will take. (To make matters worse, your trees still have a dump-truck load of leaves that will bravely hold on until the next windy day.)

If you have a nice lawn, leaves can really be a detriment to it. Late fall is still good for grass growth, and the grass needs all the sun it can get to store up energy to survive the winter. Not raking might cause the grass to lose that chance for growth, and lose its green color.

When you consider that the branches of your average tree fill an area of about forty to fifty cubic feet, and that the space is mostly filled with leaves, and that your average homeowner has at least two of these average trees on her lot, you start to realize the amount of leaves those trees could shed.

Often, most landfills have a place for disposing leaves and brush, which is separate from the garbage dump. Those leaves go into a huge compost pile. If you take the bags of leaves there yourself, you can add them to that pile.

If you're not up to bagging leaves, you might be able to mow the leaves into the lawn as they fall. Finely-chopped leaves make a great mulch for your lawn. They will decay over the winter, adding nutrients and organic material to your yard. They will cover the ground, hiding the grass roots from next summer's burning sun.

Oak leaves are much harder to mow down than maple leaves. My silver maple leaves seem to melt right into the grass. However, I have a good mulching mower, which chops leaves fine, and this mower has chewed up bags of oak leaves into a fine mulch. If you have these tough leaves, definitely look into getting a mulching mower. You'll have to go over the leaves a few times to chop them up, but it sure beats raking. Also, a good mulching mower can put between three and four inches of leaves back into the lawn.

Contrary to popular opinion, leaves don't contribute to thatch. Thatch is a condition caused by the grass roots themselves, which get too thick over the surface of the soil. Mulching the grass, with grass clippings and leaf bits, actually keeps thatch at bay. HOWEVER, if your yard already has thatch, then yes, the leaves will make the trouble worse.

There are a lot of misconceptions about thatch. Thatch is actually when the stolons and the roots of the grass grow to make a thick mat over the soil's surface. The grass does this in an attempt to mulch itself, covering its roots to protect them against the sun's heat and to keep water in. To avoid thatch, you need to let the grass clippings fall back into the lawn when you mow, and add organic material to the soil's surface. That is precisely how leaves will help.

And leaves make a super mulch for your vegetable or flower garden. One Thanksgiving morning, I dumped out seven industrial-sized bags of leaves on the garden, adding them to eight other bags of leaves. I ran the mulching mower over them, and after about a half-hour's worth of work, I had about an inch of mulch over a 15 by 25 foot area. The worms loved the mulch, too, all winter.

And the mulch is super fertilizer. You've seen how black the forest soil gets from all those leaves rotting away on its surface. Trees bring nutrients from deep underground, and many of those nutrients end up in the leaves, where they can be used on the soil's surface.

However, if your leaves are very thick, you will have to rake some of them into piles to burn, since there is only so much a mower, or a lawn, can handle.

When you get ready to burn your leaves, take several precautions. This is especially important to people living in the country, because their volunteer firefighters don't get paid a whole lot! Often in fall and spring, they're busy traveling from one end of the county to the other, trying to put out all these out-of-control blazes.

If your fire does get out of control, go on and call them. It's much easier for the firefighters, volunteer or otherwise, to contain a fire that's 20 square feet than it is to contain one that's 20 square acres.

So: Burn on calm days, since the fire can get out of control on windy days. (I've seen where a fire, started at the edge of a lawn, ended up racing across the lawn itself.) Watch the fire. Don't let burning leaves drift into your neighbor's field. Keep the fire within easy reach of the garden hose. Finally, don't burn near compost piles – those will shoot some amazing flames into the air.

After you burn your leaves, you can put the ashes in the compost pile. Ashes are high in nutrients the soil loves, and will mix well with the compost. You can also scatter them over your garden for next spring. (Don't use ashes on your garden all the time as extensive use of them will make your soil all alkaline.)

*If you grow winter crops under row covers, a thick layer of old leaves
makes a great mulch for this purpose. It holds the freezes at bay, helps
the winter crops to survive, and adds nutrients to the soil when spring
comes. And, of course, earthworms are busier than heck under this
mulch, fixing up your soil with lots of burrows and worm castings just
in time for spring. Ain't that nice of them?*
Photo by Oregon State University

My little Fothergilla getting some good mulch from the local newspaper.

MULCH THE WORLD!

Fix Out-Of-Control Weeds With Newspaper Mulch

ONE DAY THE GARDEN LOOKS just fine, and all the weeds are under control, but the next day you turn around and the neat rows of vegetables or flowers are crowded with big, hulking weeds. In the heat of summer, after a long day at work, you don't want to bust your back trying to pull or hoe all those weeds up.

Fear not. Here's a way you can knock those weeds down and keep them down. It doesn't involve chemicals that might affect your produce or damage the plants you want to keep. It is as cheap as can be, and you don't even have to pull the weeds up.

Newspapers to the rescue!

What you need are a lot of big newspapers (national papers like the *New York Times* or the *Washington Post* are good examples) and mulching materials, like grass clippings, pine bark, chopped-up leaves, straw, etc. If you don't have newspapers, go to your local library and ask for any big newspapers from their recycle bin. They'll load you up.

If the weeds are tall, walk over them to flatten them against the ground. Then open up a section of the newspaper so you have a big wide rectangle of papers, and lay them right down on the weeds. Each big rectangle of newspaper should be ten pages thick. Lay newspapers down all over the weeds, overlapping their edges so that light (and weeds) can't get through. As you lay down these papers, throw some mulch over the pages to keep them from blowing around, especially on windy days.

Bye-bye, dandelion!

If you have a lot of plants to mulch between, leave the papers folded. You can also tear the newspapers to slide them around the stems of your plants (and this is somewhat helpful in keeping cutworms at bay). Don't use glossy pages in the garden, though. Then, when the newspapers are covering the ground, lay a nice, thick layer of mulch down – about three inches – so the next thunderstorm won't pull the pages up.

And then you're done.

This does take an hour or three, depending on the size of your garden. But once you're done, the garden looks incredibly tidy and clean. And what's even better? If you've used your 10-layer-thick pages, and you've overlapped them, then you won't have to worry about weeds for the rest of the year. Occasionally a perennial weed might poke through. When that happens, move some papers out of the way, dig out the weed, cover the space with a extra square of newspaper, then re-mulch.

A newspaper mulch is a great thing to do for your garden – and for yourself.

Put a nice mulch over your newspapers, and you're all set.

An agronomist with a cabbage grown with compost! ... and a cabbage grown without. Photo courtesy of @SOILHaiti.

COMPOST – BLACK GOLD

Composting: Learn the Basics

COMPOST IS GREAT. NOT ONLY does it provide nutrients to plants, but its organic material improves the soil structure as it breaks down to become humus. Bacteria feeds on compost, producing starches that hold soil grains together; fungi also feed on it, sending "threads" through the compost to break down and absorb more of it. Both of these actions also make the soil more porous, allowing air and water to reach plant roots.

Composting is the art of letting organic materials decay into rich soil. However, sometimes composting seems much more complicated than it should be.

My composting methods are unscientific. I tend to throw stuff in the compost pile and leave it. That means I won't have finished compost for a year or two. But I'm pretty lacksadaisical.

Some people turn their piles weekly, mix the green and brown materials in equal ratios, and shred them before adding them to the pile. They keep the pile moist, and add nitrogen. These non-lacksadaisical gardeners will have finished compost in two to four months.

To compost, you need air, water, nitrogen, and, of course, stuff to compost. Spoiled vegetables, rinds and peels and cores, grass clippings, eggshells, flowers you've deadheaded, coffee grounds, old manure, and tea: all these are good for composting.

Stuff you shouldn't compost includes meat, bones, grease, oil, dairy products, and raw manure. These smell, and they invite vermin. (Naturally, there are always exceptions to the rule.)

Generally, a third of your compost should consist of fresh green materials like clippings, weeds and kitchen wastes. Another third should include dead brown materials like straw or leaves. The last third of your materials should be unfinished compost or soil. Those provide microorganisms that will break down materials. Setting your compost pile directly on the ground also provides microorganisms as well as earthworms that will help mix things up.

Rule of thumb: Green materials are fresh and juicy

(like new-cut grass), while brown materials are dried and dead (fallen leaves). Generally, if it's brown or crispy, it's a brown material.

These would be "green" materials. They aren't actually green in color – but they're juicy and full of nitrogen.

If you aren't able to keep a 50-50 ratio of greens and browns in your compost barrel, don't fret. You might keep a few bags of leaves handy so you always have enough brown materials. Of course, soon you'll have more brown material than you can handle, once fall hits, but leaves will keep.

Sometimes you don't have enough green material – just a ton of brown. In this case, mix a good source of nitrogen in with the browns. Blood meal, cottonseed meal, feathers, hoof meal and horn dust, and even hair (pick some up at the barbershop) are all good nitrogen sources.

To make composting go faster, put the materials down in layers – green, brown, and soil; green, brown, and soil; and so forth. If some of the green stuff is moldy, it's okay; fungi helps break down the compost.

Your compost needs water. When adding dried brown materials, wet them down as you put them in. The compost materials should be moist, like a wrung-out sponge. If the pile gets too wet, it will start to smell. If it's too dry, then it won't break down as fast. Think of the compost pile as a plant you need to keep watered – but don't overwater!

Next, your compost needs air. Every week, you might use a pitchfork to turn over the materials or stir them up. Some people bury drainage pipes, the ones that are shot through with holes, in the pile to let air in and out. Enclosed compost bins need air holes in the sides to let the air circulate. This is crucial for good, fast compost.

If you don't have the strength to stir, get a piece of rebar -- a metal rod used for reinforcing concrete -- or long pipe with which you can stir the pile. Wrap duct tape around the rebar so you don't burn your hand when stirring and aerating the pile. (The faster compost decomposes, the hotter it gets.) Plunge the rebar in, stir it, take it out, and tackle another spot.

The University of California has developed a way to get finished compost in 14 days. You get all your browns and greens and shred them, separately of course. Then layer them in the bin with a bit of soil or finished compost between each layer, wetting the layers (not too much!) as you do. The materials should be as moist as a squeezed-out sponge. Then get out of the way. You will need to stir the compost as it breaks down, but be careful, because it will be very hot! The compost that you get from the 14-day method will be rough, but it will be perfectly servicable.

If your compost pile refuses to get hot enough to "cook," you might try using worms. Earthworm farmers and bait shops sell earthworms that you can purchase and put in your compost heap. (Be sure the compost is not cooking when you put the worms in, of course!) Worms will help break down the compost, give you lots of valuable worm castings, and they can go into your garden with the compost to help you dig it in. Some worms won't survive the winter, but they'll work for you until then. This is basically outdoor vermiculture.

To be sure compost is well done, put a handful in a closed baggie for several days, then open it and take a whiff. Well-done compost has an earthy scent. If it's finished, take it to the garden, screen it, and add it around your plants. Some people call compost black gold. You will too, when you see how your plants grow.

Chickens on compost, breaking it down for y'all.

THE ULTIMATE IN RECYCLING: EXTREME COMPOSTING

Or, Who Put My Shirt In The Compost Pile?

I SAW A COMMERCIAL THAT SHOWED some lovers walking along a beach with the waves whooshing into the shore and some seaweed lying on the sand. I found myself fixating on that seaweed. I wanted that seaweed! Can you imagine how great that stuff would be in my compost pile? Why on earth wasn't that woman in the commercial picking it up? "Hey honey, do you know how many micronutrients this would add to my compost? Yeah, I know we're on a date, give me a hand here."

The neatest thing about compost piles (besides the obvious points – free fertilizer, free waste disposal, and the ultimate in recycling) is that, in the end, that compost pile will break down anything organic, even if it takes a while. Compost is forgiving stuff – and if something doesn't compost, well, you'll dig it out later on anyway.

When I started researching this article, I filled a bucket with compostable materials that would ordinarily go to the recycling bin or (sad to say) in the trash. This included Kleenex and paper towels, fast-food bags, Pixie Stix candy wrappers, Q-tips (cotton and paper types only), shredded bills and junk mail, graded homework papers, and cardboard tubes from the toilet paper. Pretty soon I needed a bigger bucket! Really, a lot of the cardboard and papers could have gone into the recycle bin – I just wanted to see what my compost heap could do.

Tom Fowler, University of Missouri extension agent, agrees. "Any material that is derived from plants or animals can potentially be composted. After all, using compost is the final part of the recycling process."

Naturally, as with any compost, you've got to balance the "green" materials which are high in nitrogen (vegetable peels, grass clippings, and manure) against the "brown" materials which are high in carbon (paper and cardboard, dried leaves, and hay). A 50/50 mix is good, though a 60/40 mix (more browns than greens) works best. If you have too many greens, or if the pile is too wet, the compost gets goopy and stinks. Frequently turning the pile (to add oxygen to the composting process) and adding in some browns should fix this problem. If you have too many browns, or if the pile is too dry, the compost sits there and there's not much action. But it still breaks down eventually. If we looked for perfection we'd never get anything done.

If your compost pile is too high in nitrogen, or is too wet, mix in lots of shredded papers or cardboard. These "brown materials" will add carbon and fiber and will wick out the excess moisture. Plain paper plates (not the waxy coated plates) and pizza boxes, which are forbidden in your recycling bin, are welcome in the compost. Chop up the pizza boxes, or flatten them and use them as mulch in the garden.

Clothes made of natural fibers – cotton or linen – also work in the compost pile, as well as old pillowcases and rugs. Some of the clothes take about a year to break down. A poly-cotton T-shirt will turn into a ghostly frame shirt made of poly fibers. Dryer lint and vacuum cleaner dust also break down nicely. (Synthetic fibers won't break down – they will simply be a part of the soil, inert.)

Newspapers can go into the compost – but they work better if you use them as a thick, weed-blocking mulch, as I've detailed in a previous chapter.

There is some question about whether some papers (bills, glossy newspaper inserts, laser-printed papers) add toxins or poisons to the compost. Well, not any more. These days newspapers use nontoxic and biodegradable soy inks to print their pages – the toxic stuff was banned in 1985. Also, glossy inserts are now printed with kaolin, a kind of clay also used in kitty litter. So these are now safe additions to the garden.

In the past, white paper was not good for compost due to chlorine bleaching processes, which used compounds called dioxins. However, now paper pulp is bleached through chlorine-free processes that use hydrogen peroxide or sodium dithionite. These produce benign byproducts. However, laser printers use toner, which include plastic or waxes, so you might put printed pages from the office into the recycle bin, instead of into the garden.

Old wine and beer can be composted. Dump out last night's wineglass on the pile! It's okay, microorganisms like to party too! Seriously, alcohol acts as a compost "starter," spurring the bacteria into action. If you brew your own beer or make wine, these waste products make great additions to the compost pile.

Hair, feathers, and nail clippings will add nitrogen, though they are slow to break down. If you have lot of hair, scatter it through the compost. Hair will mat together if you leave it in a big pile.

Fruit peels and old vegetable bits add nitrogen as well as a little phosphorus and potash. Coffee grounds (with filters) and tea bags are good for acid-loving plants, and they add trace elements to the mix. Cotton, felt, leather, rawhide, and wool add nitrogen to the pile, as well as silk and linen. Be patient while you wait for these things to break down.

When you clean your fish tank, dump the dirty water onto the compost pile to give the microorganisms in the pile a boost. Algae from your pond is good. Seaweed is even better. Be sure to wash the salt off before you add it to the pile, but your plants will love these trace minerals.

Bones can be composted if you have a very hot pile that you turn daily. After three weeks in a hot pile, bones become soft, like putty.

Now, this article is about composting *everything* – so if you are the sensitive type, you might just skip the next two paragraphs ....

Urine is a great compost activator. It's high in nitrogen and, er, readily spreadable. So if you have a nice compost pile that's not very hot, and you don't have any gawking neighbors – well, there you go. A few of you are probably familiar with "humanure," and so you know that you can use shredded paper as the "sawdust" in a pee-only sawdust toilet, which can be as simple as a five-gallon bucket. When the bucket is ready, open up a pit in your compost pile, layer in the humanure, and cover it up. If you Google "sawdust toilet," you can find more information about how to set up your own bucket toilet with a minimum of fuss. (Note: Avoid doing this if you use pharmaceuticals – which will end up in your garden.)

And, while we're on the topic: tampons and menstrual pads are compostable only if they are made of unbleached cotton. Cardboard tampon applicators and latex condoms are also compostable.

Well, I did say that this article is about composting *everything.*

If you're thinking about dumping your ashtray into the compost, don't. Tobacco can carry tobacco mosaic disease, which is spread by a virus that can survive temperatures of 150 degrees Fahrenheit – AND can survive in dried plant parts for 50 years or more. That little fire on the end of your cigarette does not affect the virus. Composting any tobacco products is out.

Large amounts of grease and used cooking oil shouldn't be composted because they suffocate microorganisms, repel water, and attract unwanted critters. (Small, infrequent amounts of oil are okay, but mix it into the pile so you don't create an anaerobic lump of gunk.) Wax (such as cheese rinds or in candles) can be composted, even beeswax. Or earwax for that matter. Wax will take a long time to break down, though.

Fruitcake is compostable.

If dogs, cats, or rats roam your neighborhood, bury your turkey carcasses and chicken bones in the ground instead of composting them. If you have a fish fry, bury the fish bones next to your rosebush or in the corn, and send that nitrogen and calcium straight to the roots.

Don't compost dog and cat waste, since this could spread diseases to you (particularly toxoplasmosis). Also, kitty litter, which is made of kaolinite clay, will turn to cement in the compost heap. The best thing to do is to make a small, covered pit away from the garden to dump the pet waste in, topping it off with leaves, straw, soil, or lime. When the pit is nearly full, cover it with soil and dig a new one.

Animal carcasses (roadkill, chicken parts, etc.) are fine if you have a hot pile. Dead critters are good compost activators. One compost enthusiast regularly composts cows and horses, though he also has a front-loader and some gigantic compost piles as big as houses. So it can be done!

Shells and seafood scraps take a while to break down. After they spend some time in the sun and rain, they'll shatter if you whack them with a hoe.

Weeds are good to compost. Weed seeds are not, especially if your compost tends to break down slowly – a hot pile can kill the seeds but a cool pile will not.

Plants infected with common garden diseases should be disposed away from the garden, since the temperatures of a home pile won't kill some disease pathogens (see: tobacco mosaic virus).

Now, if you do put some small amount of these forbidden substances in your compost by mistake, don't sweat it. Doing something that's "against the rules" is not going to make your compost heap explode. We're dealing with the raw materials of dirt. Dirt is forgiving: after all, it's put up with us all this time.

Now, there are downsides to composting everything. If you have a cold or slow pile, then things won't break down very fast. You might also get some less than enjoyable results: noxious smells, dogs dragging out your roadkill during a dinner party, surprise maggots, or drunken raccoons enjoying that bad wine you dumped out.

You will have to screen your compost before you use it, or odd things will turn up in your garden – threads, a jean jacket skeleton, Legos, a duck bill.

But the upside? Great soil, the great feeling of knowing that you are saving good materials from everlasting consignment in landfills, and a little nerdy fun.

The results of excellent garden soil: Godzilla cabbage!

SIXTY WEIRD THINGS YOU CAN COMPOST!

1) Paper bag
2) Drywall and plaster
3) Fruit and vegetable scraps
4) Q-tips and cotton balls (real cotton only)
5) Weeds
6) Small twigs and leaves
7) Corn-based plastic
8) Paper towels, tissues, napkins and toilet paper
9) Hair or pet hair
10) Dryer lint
11) Vacuum cleaner bags and contents
12) Beer and wine (these also act as compost activators)
13) Leavings from making beer or wine
14) Old shirts, jeans, underwear, etc.
15) Cloth: Cotton, linen, silk, felt, and wool
16) Wine corks (real cork only)
17) Seaweed/kelp/algae
18) Skulls and bones
19) Meat scraps
20) Shredded paper
21) Shredded bills
22) Newspaper (including glossies)
23) Wasp nests

24) Nail clippings

25) Paper plates and cups (no wax)

26) Pizza boxes and egg cartons (no Styrofoam cartons)

27) Wool clothing of any kind

28) Pencil shavings

29) Roadkill

30) Ashes from grill or fireplace (in limited amounts)

31) Burlap bags

32) Old rope (no synthetic rope)

33) Used masking tape

34) Old leather (such as gardening gloves)

35) Cardboard tampon applicators and latex condoms

36) Cardboard tubes from gift wrap, paper towels, toilet paper.

37) Old pet food

38) Used loofahs (plant-based ones, not plastic)

39) Crepe paper streamers

40) Cotton batting

41) Urine (use in moderation)

42) Water hyacinths

43) Ragged washcloths or dishtowels (cotton only)

44) Expired food out of the pantry

45) Old paperback novels with the covers torn off

46) Ivory soap (99 44/100 percent pure!)

47) Corncobs (these will take forever)

48) Rawhide and pig's ears (for dogs)

49) Milk that's gone bad

50) Old cheese

51) Sun Chips bags (they will rattle around in the compost for at least a year)

52) Hamster or rabbit cage leavings

53) Feathers and down

54) Dirt from sweeping

55) Extra sourdough starter

56) Shells (mussel, oyster, clam, etc.)

57) Little bitty bones

58) Pizza crusts

59) Nutshells (cracked in little pieces)

60) Cloth scraps from quilting

Brown compostables also make a great place for your cat to sit in the sun.

MORE BASIC ORGANIC SOIL AMENDMENTS

NOW, NOT EVERYBODY WANTS TO PUT their old underwear and stale potato chips in the compost. Not everybody goes for the "everything but the kitchen sink" approach (also, porcelain takes forever to break down and should be pulverized before adding to the compost). So here is a list of the more traditional organic soil amendments that you can add to your compost, to your mulch, or straight into your soil, and you won't be haunted by their ghosts over a year from now.

But there are tons of other ingredients you can add to

the ground to improve it.

Tons, people. TONS.

Read on!

Basic slag – If you have a smelting plant near your home, you might be able to get your hands on this. Basic slag is created when iron ore is smelted to create pig iron. All kinds of elements can be found in trace amounts in basic slag, including lime, iron, magnesia, and silica. Get the finely pulverized stuff. If you have an acidic soil that you need to sweeten, use slag instead of lime. Apply it in autumn and winter. Avoid slags that have a lot of sulphur.

Bird cage cleanings –These are good nitrogen sources, and bring along the old newspapers, feathers, and seeds! A little bit of these will get a compost pile going, and quickly.

Blood meal – Pick blood meal up at the feed store or at your local retailer. This has a high nitrogen content. Use this in the ground or compost it. It's supposed to keep rabbit away – sometimes it work, sometimes it doesn't. Bury it, though, because it really interests dogs and cats.

Bone meal – The same goes for bone meal. I left a bag outside one day while I went inside for a glass of water. When I looked out the window I saw Brownie, the neighborhood dog, gnawing on the bag and tearing it open as if there were dog candy inside. A great source of phosphorus with a little nitrogen, though I'm sure Brownie was interested only in the taste.

Raw bone meal is slow to decay due to the fat that it contains. Steamed bone meal is the kind you usually see at the stores. Mix bone meal with other organic materials for best results. This will sweeten the soil, too.

Buckwheat hulls – These take a long time to break down, so use them as a mulch.

Cocoa bean shells – Also a better mulch material. Also, it smells nice, so that you have to go to the store and buy a candy bar.

Coffee wastes – If you're addicted to coffee, then you have a lot of good stuff to send to the compost pile. Put your used grounds around acid-loving plants like blueberries, magnolias, and azaleas. If you have plants that prefer alkaline soils, mix the grounds with a little lime. Coffee grounds seem to stimulate the growth of some plants. Must be all that caffeine. On the other hand, maybe caffeine does not stimulate growth, because if it did I'd be 58 feet tall by now.

Cottonseed meal – It's good for plants that like acid soils, and is a good source of nitrogen. You might lay this on top of the soil and put a heavier mulch on top to keep it moist and help it break down. Cottonseed meal, when used as a mulch, sheds water – or it did when I used it.

Epsom salts – The magnesium in this stops blossom-end rot in tomatoes, and it encourages basal breaks in roses, which allows roses to grow new canes. Put a half-cup around each plant every month.

Fish bits – If you've been fishing and have finished filleting your fish, take the stinky parts and bury them in the garden and water them in. Then you'll grow a fish tree! No, actually, fish bits are great for plants. It's said that when the Seneca planted corn, they put a fish in the soil by every plant. It works for roses, too. But water the ground after planting fish so you wash away the fish smell and the animals don't dig it up.

Fish emulsion – The cats will come running when you start watering your plants with this! And all the flies will come to pay you a visit! But emulsion is an excellent source of nitrogen and the plants love it, especially roses.

Garbage (composted) – Of course! Kitchen wastes, old Halloween pumpkins, dryer lint and used tissues (these work better in a moist compost heap), hair, sawdust sweepings from the shop floor, leftover beer, algae and extra water plants from the fish pond (water hyacinth is a super-multiplier plant that goes well in the compost heap), tea bags, etc. Compost them all!

Grass clippings – One of our most underused sources of compost and mulch. High in nitrogen, easy to spread out. Clippings make my eyes water and my nose clog up, but I still love 'em. Use them as a fast-decaying mulch in the garden, or just take the bag off and let them fall into the yard to fertilize the grass. If you use them as green material for the compost heap, keep the layer of clippings thin or they turn into stinky muck. Also, layer them with composted manure and brown materials for best results.

Greensand (or marl) – This is an undersea deposit that contains many of the nutrients and minerals you'd find in seawater. It's an especially good source of potash. The plants enjoy all the trance minerals found in greensand. Apply this at about a quarter-pound per square foot of soil. Super for lawns; just use the spreader. Use in the garden or in the compost pile.

Leaves – Trees bring up nutrients from deep in the subsoil which end up in the leaves. Contains twice as many minerals as manure, and they improve soil structure. They can be hard to compost, though. Chop up the leaves by running over them again and again with a lawnmower (a mulching mower works best) then compost by mixing with manure or some other high-nitrogen additive (5 parts leaves to 1 part manure) and keep the pile moist! Or use the chopped leaves as a mulch in the garden, or till it into the soil. Or gather the leaves in a big pile, wetting them down as you do, and just let them break down on their own over several years, until they make a rich loam. Moisture helps them break down.

Limestone – You use this as a soil conditioner to raise the pH, instead of as a fertilizer. Legumes really like lime. Lime also opens up clay soils and causes them to release more elements to the plants. Use 50 pounds per 1000 square feet every 3 to 4 years, and the lime will percolate slowly down into the soil.

Manure – You can use manure from nearly any animal except from dogs and cats, since they may transmit diseases that could affect humans. Manure should be stored in a way to keep nitrogen from leaching away – for instance, cover the compost pile loosely with a tarp to keep rain out but to let air in. You can visit a cattle farmer, or go to a stables where horses are kept.

They'll even load up your truck with a skid loader if you like. You might even ask about getting manure delivered. Sometimes they want so badly to get rid of a pile they'll do anything!

Poultry manure is good, too, though it gets hot very quickly, since it's so high in nitrogen. It's excellent for getting your compost pile started.

We have a surprise for you!
It's poop.

Peat moss – In Europe, you shouldn't use peat moss because much of the supply is from the rapidly-dwindling peat fields in and around England. In America, the supply comes from Canada, which has plenty, so it's okay (or has been so far).

Peat moss doesn't add much nutrition to the soil. Instead, it's used to make the soil more crumbly and looser. Not for the compost heap; add it directly to the soil and till it in.

Sawdust – Best used as a mulch, though it may take nitrogen away from the plants as it decays. Add some blood meal or other high-nitrogen additive and water to balance it out. Sawdust doesn't sour the soil all that much, but if you're worried about it, add a little lime. Also, be sure that the sawdust is from untreated lumber only! Some lumber is treated with arsenic, and that's something you don't want to put down among your cucumbers.

Seaweed – I live a thousand miles from the ocean and I wish I could get my hands on some of this. Compost this with manure and then use it on your crops. Don't let it sit in the open without protection because its minerals may leach out.

Straw – This is common and easy to use. If you compost it, mix it with "green" materials (fresh grass clippings, algae, manure, etc.) to get it to break down quickly. Straw makes a great mulch, too.

Sewage sludge – I would not recommend this, because most sludge has heavy metals from industrial wastes in it, in a concentrated form. However, the sludge might be okay if it's treated through a biological process, such as a sand filter or a trickling filter, or if it's activated sludge.

Sugar beet wastes – Those make good silage if you have livestock, but good for the compost heap, too. It provides mostly potash to the soil, with a little N and P thrown in, with trace amounts of calcium and magnesium.

Tea and coffee grounds – These contain nitrogen, and make a super mulch for acid-loving plants. They seem to stimulate growth in some plants, too.

Garbanzo beans (aka chickpeas) grown as a cover crop.
Photo credit: USDA NRCS Montana

GREEN MANURES AND COVER CROPS

IMAGINE GROWING A BLANKET OF PLANTS that return quick nutrients to your garden – plants that you can use as mulch, or to restore your soil. This is what green manures do. Green manures are plants you use specifically to make the soil more fertile.

You can get all the benefits of green manures while making full use of your vegetable garden, because there are plenty of ways to tuck these into your fertility program!

The terms "cover crops" and "green manures" are often used interchangeably, but both have different purposes. Cover crops are grown to cover the ground and to break up the soil. Cover crops are generally skimmed off with a shovel at the end of their growing season and used as a mulch, or used to fortify the compost pile. At the end of a green manure's growing season, these plants are turned under.

These plants help immeasurably with soil building. Deep-rooting plants such as alfalfa, sweet clover, or lupines can really break into the subsoil. Daikon radishes open up compacted soils; when allowed to rot in the ground, they allow air into the soil and add organic material where you really need it. And of course you can eat them.

Often, legumes are used for both cover crops and green manures. Legumes put a nice bit of nitrogen into the soil. They smother weeds, help suppress weed seed germination, and even suppress pathogenic nematodes.

Legumes such as clovers, chickpeas, and beans will fix nitrogen in the soil. Plants that aren't legumes are still useful – they will trap the nitrogen in of the soil that would otherwise leach away. Then, when you plow them under or add them to the compost pile, they'll return the nitrogen to where you want it.

Sowing a cover crop or green manure is fairly straightforward. Prepare your seedbed by tilling or hoeing it up, breaking the soil into a fine tilth, and remove the weeds. Sow the seeds widely for good coverage, so when they come up they'll suppress the weeds. Larger seeds, such as field beans or forage peas, can be sown in furrows a couple of inches apart, in rows that are about six inches apart. Once all the seeds are sown, lightly rake over the seedbed and water it well. Keep watering it until your little seedlings pop up and get established.

Cover Crops and Their Benefits

Cover crops are great to put down in fall to hold the soil in place and avoid erosion. In spring, you can skim the cover crops off with a flat shovel, put down some compost, and plant your crops right over the roots. This works only if you have planted an annual cover crop, because a perennial cover crop will resprout right into your lettuces.

Don't use forage rye or winter tares in places where you intend to sow seeds, unless you can leave the ground fallow for four weeks after you skim them off. These two plants release chemicals that inhibit seed germination. Use them in places where you want to inhibit weed seed growth.

Later in the season, as you harvest your crops, you can grow cover crops in fallow areas. For instance, once the early crops, such as lettuce and peas, are finished, then sow the cover crop seeds and let them grow through the summer. On occasion you could skim off the green growth and use it as mulch.

Cover crops bring in bees and other beneficial insects, giving them nectar to drink and a place to live. This will drastically reduce, or even end, your use of insecticides. Cover crops also act as a living mulch, keeping the soil cool during the hot summer. The soil doesn't dry out so readily. Weed seeds have a more difficult time germinating. It's just useful all around!

Green Manures and Their Benefits

Green manures are grown, then cut down. You let them wilt in place for a day before tilling them in. That slows the plants' breakdown in the soil.

In fall, after you harvest, seed your garden area with green manures. These plants will capture nutrients that would otherwise leach away over the winter. Four to six weeks before planting season starts, till them into the soil. You could also plant green manures in spring to be tilled under before the planting season starts in late summer. Be sure to remember that green manures take about four to six weeks to break down in the ground, and they will tie up some nitrogen while they're decomposing.

Green manures will not make your garden into a powerhouse producer in one season. As a rule, green manures don't add a lot of permanent organic matter. But it will add enough organic material for the soil to use immediately, and it will increase yields. Also, legumes are super at putting the nitrogen right in the soil where your plants need it most. If you use legumes right, you don't need to add nitrogen to the soil at all. Be sure that the soil has enough molybdenum and cobalt – these are trace elements that help the plants fix nitrogen.

Plants to use as green manures include sweet clover, Ladino clover, alfalfa, trefoil, buckwheat, rye (this is considered the best), redtop, and timothy.

Where To Plant Them

Underplanting is a good way to use legumes. Often, if you sow them in the fall after you clear out the garden, they don't have time to get established before the freezes hit. Here's another way to use legumes: Plant your regular crops first, give the crops four or five weeks head start, then sow legumes around the crops. By then the crops are big enough to not be overwhelmed by your cover crops, and the legumes still have room to grow. When the crops are harvested, let the legumes keep growing. If they get too big, clip them with a weed whacker or run the lawnmower over them.

If you're going to be using your green manures over

the summer, sow a mix of legumes with grasses. Many legumes peter out during the hot weather, and when they do, grasses can take up the slack.

Grow low plants like white clover in walkways. Once it's established, it will take your foot traffic with no trouble. You might make your garden walkways just wide enough for your lawnmower so when you mow the yard, you can take the mower right down the walkways, scattering bits of clover all over the garden where it will be used by the plants. Also, clover attracts the bees that will pollinate your plants. White clover is a perennial, so it will come up year after year. You will have to keep it within bounds so it doesn't reseed and spread into your other garden beds. Some people aren't up to the task of fighting clover – so in those cases, the benefits aren't worth the extra work.

Plants to Use

Protip: Be sure to mow or shear these cover crops and green manures before they go to seed, because many of these plants can reseed rapidly! Also, once they start flowering, the plants turn woody and then it's a real chore to cut them down and till them in.

Winter rye is a bit slow to get started, but once it does, it grows quickly, and greens up nicely in spring. This is about the only green manure you can plant after the vegetable garden is done and it will be able to grow and survive the winter, in northern climates of course.

Hairy, or winter, vetch, is a good source of nitrogen.

Buckwheat is good for bringing in honeybees. You get a lot of rapid, lush growth. It's good to use this if you have a garden area sitting idle for a month or more. It doesn't mind hot weather, either.

Weeds can also be used as cover crops or green manure. Just be sure that none of them are perennial weeds, and please be sure to get them cut down before they go to seed!

Daikon radishes are great for breaking up the soil. They have wide, long roots. You can also eat them.

Beets, radishes, and turnips, are good to break up the soil, and you can eat them too. Roots from these can go down from five to seven feet deep, so they help break up the subsoil.

Clover, Alsike Clover, Crimson Clover, Red Clover, Alfalfa Clover

Legumes – to see if they're fixing nitrogen in the soil, take a nodule (a small knot on the roots) and open it with your fingernail. If the nodule is pink on the inside, then the plant is doing its magic.

Soybeans, alfalfa, any clover, vetch, are all good

legumes. Alfalfa should be used for a longer-term cover crop instead of a green manure. Be sure to trim it before it blooms, which can be three or four times a year. Once it blooms the stems turn woody and hard to clip.

Cultivé dans les champs. — Fleurit de juin en septembre.

Luzerne cultivée.
Medicago sativa.
— LÉGUMINEUSES. —

ALFALFA: A GARDENER'S SECRET INGREDIENT

ALFALFA, ALSO KNOWN AS "The Queen of Forages," has been used by farmers for millennia. Because the bulk of its roots reach five to eight feet deep, fixing nitrogen in the soil, alfalfa has been the farmer's favorite for loosening up soils and restoring their fertility.

In the last few years, alfalfa's benefits have been dawning on the home gardener – and it's about time. Alfalfa contains an alcohol called triacontanol, a stimulant that makes roses pop with new growth. The first time I added a fertilizer that contained alfalfa to the soil around my roses and watered it in, I couldn't believe all the new shoots that shot out. Not that I was complaining!

Alfalfa is great in the vegetable and perennial garden, too. The Organic Gardening Research Center found that small amounts of triacontanol increased vegetable yields by 30 to 60 percent. Alfalfa also contains trace minerals such as iron, potassium, and magnesium that enrich the soil. These nutrients and elements are slowly released to the plant, so they don't leach away after a rainstorm.

To get the most benefit from alfalfa, the small gardener would do well to grow a few alfalfa plants in her garden as a small hedge, perhaps next to the corn. This way, one can grow perennial alfalfa for several years, thereby getting the benefit of its deep roots breaking up garden subsoil, plus its nitrogen-fixing abilities.

Start the hedge in August or September next to any fall crops you plan to grow over the winter. By winter you'll have a small windbreak to help hold the wind off your cold-season crops. Or, grow the hedge where your corn grew, and replace the nutrients that the corn took from the soil.

The gardener can clip the alfalfa hedge, since the plant should be cut back every 28 days anyway, and harvest the leaves for mulch on the garden topsoil. Just before the first purple flowers open, get a pair of hedge shears and cut the alfalfa plants down to eight or 10 inches tall. Snip the plants little by little to make lots of small, scatterable bits instead of a couple of big parts. Then rake or throw the alfalfa over the garden as a growth-enhancing, high-nitrogen mulch suppliment. Keep the clippings scattered – if there are too many in one place, they will mat and shed water.

Harvest alfalfa when the plant is dry. Wet alfalfa clippings could spread mosaic to your legumes and to other mosiac-susceptible plant. (Actually, it's a good rule of thumb to never touch or cut any plant when it's wet, because diseases and pathogens are readily transmitted by water.)

Harvest the alfalfa plants in this way every 28 days. Don't skip a cutting, because then the stems turn woody and you just about need an axe to chop it down. Stop harvesting perennial alfalfa in September so its roots can store carbohydrates for the winter. Put several inches of mulch over the crown of the plant to help the plant survive the winter.

An alfalfa hedge should not be grown near potatoes or tomatoes. The excess nitrogen would cause too much green growth, which in turn will cause fruit production to slow down. The best place for such a hedge would be next to the corn, or other leaf crops such as lettuce, cabbage, and herbs – these need the nitrogen to produce juicy, succulent leaves. Keep in mind that any plants grown near alfalfa will need more water because alfalfa can dry out the soil with all of its roots.

Be warned: when alfalfa is grown as a perennial, its roots will be so fibrous that a tiller will not be able to chop them up. When the plants die off, or after you kill them off, you will have to plant in that area without tilling. Here's how: Lay an organic mulch over the alfalfa roots, such as shredded leaves and grass, about two or three inches thick. Plant the seeds in the mulch as if it were soil. The seeds will come up in the mulch, and their roots will make their own arrangements with the ground – willingly, due to all the nitrogen there for the taking. Once the young plants start growing, keep throwing mulch around their roots all through their growing season.

Don't plant other legumes where alfalfa has recently grown, because they will share diseases through the soil. Also, it's more helpful to the garden soil to plant legume-fixing nitrogen in more than one place.

To use alfalfa as a green manure, sow an annual alfalfa (not perennial) in August or September and let it grow through the fall and winter. (The seeds will need to be inoculated before sowing if legumes have not recently grown in the garden; rhizobium bacteria inoculum should be available at most local feed stores.) Then, next spring, three weeks before spring planting begins, mow the alfalfa down and till it under. This will give the alfalfa time to decompose before your vegetable seeds start germinating.

Alfalfa in the garden can also be harvested, in small quantities, as a healthy supplement to some diets.

Alfalfa sprouts are quick to grow and high in antioxidant activity. The young leaves of the alfalfa plant contains vitamins A, D, E, K, tons of vitamin C, and is said to have curative effects on people with diabetes? The big downside is that the leaves are not very tasty. Eat alfalfa leaves in moderation, because over-consumption can cause lupus in some people. If you already have lupus, skip the alfalfa altogether.

Alfalfa tea retains all these good properties, but it tastes like boiled socks. Mix the alfalfa with peppermint leaves to make it more palatable.

There are a few drawbacks with alfalfa. Alfalfa will not grow in soils with a pH lower than 6.5 unless lime is added; the lower pH immobilizes the nitrogen-fixing bacteria that occur in the nodules. Also fewer soil nutrients are available to the alfalfa plant at that lower pH. In northern areas, alfalfa can also be invasive and hard to get rid of if it goes to seed. (Alfalfa rarely goes to seed south of zone 4.) Alfalfa needs a lot of phosphorus and potassium, which is available in bonemeal and greensand.

Alfalfa plants have their share of pests, including alfalfa weevils. Potato leafhoppers and spider mites will attack the plants in dry years. Before the pests get really bad, cut down the alfalfa and throw it on the compost heap, mix it with equivalent amounts of dirt and brown materials, water it until it's moist, and let the compost cook.

Don't plant alfalfa in the same place twice, because it will not grow well, a condition called autotoxicity. You can replant after several years have passed.

Tips For Starting Alfalfa Plants

A half-pound of alfalfa seed should be more than enough for a small home garden, unless you really love those alfalfa sprouts. In that case, go to town.

Inoculate the seeds with rhizobium bacteria made specifically for alfalfa, or the plants won't grow very well. Be sure the inoculant is fresh. Plant the seeds no deeper than a half-inch, though one can get by with three-quarters of an inch in sandy soils. Or, plant them in a finely-chopped mulch at the same depth to avoid tilling or digging! Give each plant at least 15 inches of space. Once the young plants have grown to about six inches, add some more mulch around them to keep their roots cool and moist.

A nice little no-till setup for a home garden.

NO-TILL GARDENING

No-Till Gardens Are Good For Worms and the Soil Food Web.

SURPRISE, YOU REALLY DON'T HAVE to till every year. It may actually be better for the soil if you don't till. The worms and the tiny creatures that live in the soil are building tunnels that aerate the soil; the worms leave castings that improve the fertility of the soil. (You can buy worm castings – $4.99 for a quart – but it's far better to have the worms already in the garden!) Tilling the soil destroys these habitats, and the worms have to work to make a comeback, instead of working to improve your soil. This goes for vegetable gardens, too.

Worms are also a barometer of your garden's health. More worms equals a more fertile garden. Add organic material every year, but till every few years.

After you add all the good stuff and rake it smooth, cover everything with a three-inch layer of mulch. (By spring the mulch will have settled to two inches.) Worms like the mulch – and so will the plants. Mulch will keep the ground from heaving during freeze/thaw cycles, keeps it from drying out, and protects the foliage of the perennials.

Tilling is overrated. It kills off many earthworms that could be doing the digging for you. Happy earthworms make a happy garden. If you till every five to seven years, instead of every year, you could keep moving your alfalfa around the garden as part of your normal crop rotation, eventually enriching the soil and loosening the subsoil all over the garden patch.

FIXING LOUSY SOIL

Everybody Hates Subdivision Soil

IF YOUR HOUSE IS NEWLY built, or you've moved into a new housing development, your soil probably will be atrocious, made of subsoil and heavy clay, and there may be too much water from sprinklers and not enough drainage. I call this "subdivision soil," and it's a bear to work with, and it quickly kills off trees. Recently I drove through a subdivision, one built within the last five years. The lawns looked nice, the houses were all lovely and tidy, but I saw so many dead or dying young trees.

I first saw subdivision soil close up when I worked at a local landscaping company. We had to plant in a new housing development. That soil was the worst I'd seen outside of the soil at Felix Street Square (and you must remember, a whole building used to stand there). Under the sod was pure clay, both yellow and gray, filled with rock that the shovel would strike against, which was jarring. Once in a while, we'd dig up an area of plants that had been turned under, rotting without the help of air – phew!

Due to the compaction of the soil, drainage was nonexistent. You could see that in white pines that had been planted earlier – the pines showed great gaps in their foliage, and you could easily see the trunks and branches. White pines hate poorly drained soil.

You can also see the effects of bad soil at Felix Street Square, which has about a foot to 17 inches of soil that can be dug and then a layer of compacted hardpan that a jackhammer might get into but not a shovel.

So, I'm going to dig that soil out of the garden at Felix Street Square. That awful clay soil is among the worst I have ever seen. It has got to go! So it will.

The digging is the fun part.

(It's not really fun.)

But it is fun when you consider the end result -- beautiful soil, happy plants, my gosh, I could actually have a decent garden here! So I dig, slicing into the clay, bending the knees to heft the soil into the truck bed, then set the shovel into the soil again, about nine inches deep.

Once in a while I have to lean on the shovel and catch my breath, muscles aching. Wow. How can I move all this dirt? But it's satisfying, seeing it go. I can see the work I'm accomplishing. Sometimes, when I work on a story (or this column), it's hard to keep going because I don't ever feel like I'm getting anywhere -- I'm just floundering in words and making a mess. But when I dig a big hole in the ground, I can see the results (and if I'm not careful, I can fall in it).

At the day's end, I dump the compost in and rake it out. It is a rich, dark brown. The part of the garden I haven't been able to finish digging up is a pasty yellow color. When I get all this soil replaced, I'm going to be a happy lady.

I'm also going to be built like Arnold Schwarzenegger.

Add Good Things to Improve Your Soil

So I was talking to my Grandma Ann (okay, more like complaining) about the awful soil at Felix Street Square. "How do you improve your soil without all that digging?" Grandma Ann asked.

That's a good question. I've been pondering it myself, because after having shoveled all that bad clay muck out of the Felix Street Square garden, I am sick and tired of digging. I've dug out enough clay hardpan and shoveled enough compost for this year, thank you very much!

Soil is fascinating (when you're not digging in it). The soil's ecosystem is teeming with worms, ants, bacteria (many of which are good – even the bacteria on your hands), protozoa, springtails, miles and miles of fungi, moles and voles – the list goes on and on. All of these creatures enrich the soil in one way or another.

Worms are a good indicator of how alive your soil is. If you don't see many worms when you dig, your soil may need help.

Some sources actually say that it's best not to dig too much, because excessive digging and tilling can tear apart the ecosystems that already exist in the soil. I can get behind that theory.

So, how do you improve the soil?

First, get a soil test from the University Extension Center to find out what the soil needs – or doesn't need. They have information about how to take a soil test and how to read the results.

Next, use a pitchfork, or put on a pair of cleats, and punch holes in the ground for aeration.

Then add the good stuff. An inch-thick layer of compost or well-rotted manure works wonders, releasing nutrients over the long term. Use bone meal to add phosphorus or blood meal to add nitrogen.

Enviro-Max, a product being sold at local nurseries, helps open pores in the soil that allow the soil to breathe. You spray it on the ground, then water it in deeply.

Finally, compost tea feeds your soil ecosystem and increases fertility. Put some compost in an old sock, tie off the end, and soak it in a bucket of rainwater for several days. Pour that on the garden and then step back. Your plants will love it.

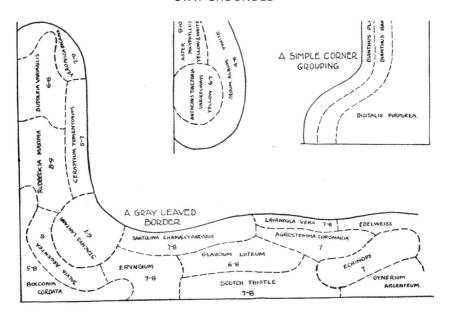

HOW TO MAKE A NEW GARDEN BED

And, How To Improve A Very Sad Garden Soil.

BECAUSE SOMETIMES YOU JUST need a new garden!

A fairly simple way to start a new garden bed is to mark the boundaries of the garden plot, then lay 2 or 3 inches of organic matter - composted manure, rich compost, shredded leaves, etc. - over the area. Add a liberal dusting of bone meal (put up the dogs before you do, lest they get all excited about it), then haul out the tiller.

Till the ground several times in different directions to mix it all up and get the organic matter deep into the soil.

When you're done, the garden area will be raised several inches above the ground around it, but that's OK; don't worry about tamping it down. Instead, give it a good layer of mulch -- shredded leaves (run them over with the lawnmower, or they will clump together), wood chips, even shredded newspaper and office paper. Then let the microorganisms in the soil do the work all winter. By spring, the soil will have settled, the organic matter will have worked itself well into the soil's structure, and you will have a place for your plants, ready to go.

For the already-established garden, give the plants a good soaking, then give them a little mulch. Pull up annuals and cut back perennials when they turn black; add them to the mulch, too. When the ground freezes, add several more inches of mulch to protect the ground from the occasional freeze-thaw that can mess roots up.

But be careful: if your house is newly built, or in a new housing development, your soil probably will be atrocious, and there may be too much water from sprinklers as well as not enough drainage. This quickly kills off trees. Recently I drove through a subdivision, one built within the last five years. The lawns looked nice, the houses were all lovely and tidy, but I saw so many dead or dying young trees.

I first saw subdivision soil close up when I worked at Caretaker's. We had to plant in a new housing development. That soil was the worst I'd seen outside of the soil at Felix Street Square (and you must remember, a building used to stand there). Under the sod was pure clay, both yellow and gray, filled with rock that the shovel would strike against, which was jarring. Once in a while, we'd dig up an area of plants that had been turned under, rotting without the help of air -- phew!

Due to the compaction of the soil, drainage was nonexistent. You could see that in white pines that had been planted earlier -- the pines showed great gaps in their foliage, and you could easily see the trunks and branches. White pines hate poorly drained soil.

You can also see the effects of bad soil at Felix Street Square, which has about a foot to 17 inches of soil that can be dug and then a layer of compacted hardpan that a jackhammer might get into but not a shovel.

But if your environment is bad, don't lose hope. Plant trees that do better in boggy conditions (such as bald cypress, if you have the space for it), and avoid trees that hate poor drainage, such as white pines and redbuds.

Raised Garden Beds To Save The Soil (And Your Back)

You can also put in raised beds, bermed with landscaping pavers, rocks, or landscape timbers. Stack up your edging materials – it doesn't need to be too high. Then lay a thick layer of newspapers at the bottom, and cover those with well-shredded leaves. Finally, fill the area up with topsoil and compost and other organic materials. Then plant. When you get the plants up out of the bad soil, they get the benefit of good soil AND good drainage.

Then, while you're growing a garden up above the soil, worms and microorganisms can work on the bad soil below your raised bed. Bring in nightcrawlers to dig those deep burrows that the soil below so desperately needs.

Nº 23.
ANNELIDA TERRICOLA.
Earth-worms.

Earth-worms out on their grassy knoll, having a party, as earth-worms do.

THE END

FREE PREVIEWS OF MY OTHER GARDENING BOOKS

Here's a preview of *Don't Throw in the Trowel: Vegetable Gardening Month by Month.*

Two things:

First: You know more about gardening than you think.

Second: A garden – the soil – plants – all of these are very forgiving. When it comes down to it, you can make a lot of mistakes and still come out with good results.

Don't Throw in the Trowel: Vegetable Gardening Month by Month, includes info on seeds, transplanting, growing, and harvesting, as well as diseases, garden pests, and organic gardening. I also talk about garden prep, because a good plan, a garden notebook, and a little off-season work will save you a lot of trouble down the road.

I've worked in horticulture for 20 years: in landscape design and installation, as a greenhouse tech, perennial manager, and city horticulturist & rosarian. This book shares what I've learned so far.

Save Time and Trouble with Garden Journals

When I worked as a municipal horticulturist, I took care of twelve high-maintenance gardens, and a number of smaller ones, over I-don't-know-how-many square miles of city, plus several hundred small trees, an insane number of shrubs, a greenhouse, and whatever else the bosses threw at me. I had to find a way to stay organized besides waking up at 3 a.m. to make extensive lists. My solution: keep a garden journal.

Vegetable gardeners with an organized journal can take control of production and yields. Whether you have a large garden or a small organic farm, it certainly helps to keep track of everything in order to beat the pests, make the most of your harvest, and keep up with spraying and fertilizing.

Keeping a garden journal reduces stress because your overtaxed brain won't have to carry around all those lists. It saves time by keeping you focused. Writing sharpens the mind, helps it to retain more information, and opens your eyes to the world around you.

My journal is a small five-section notebook, college ruled, and I leave it open to the page I'm working on at the time. The only drawback with a spiral notebook is that after a season or two I have to thumb through a lot of pages to find an earlier comment. A small three-ring binder with five separators would do the trick, too. If you wish, you can take out pages at the end of each season and file them in a master notebook.

I keep two notebooks – one for ornamentals and one for vegetables. However, you might prefer to pile everything into one notebook. Do what feels comfortable to you.

These are the five sections I divide my notebooks into – though you might use different classifications, or put them in different orders. Don't sweat it; this ain't brain surgery. Feel free to experiment. You'll eventually settle into the form that suits you best.

First section: To-do lists.

This is pretty self-explanatory: you write a list, you cross off almost everything on it, you make a new list.

When I worked as horticulturist, I did these lists monthly. I'd visit all the gardens I took care of. After looking at anything left unfinished on the previous month's list, and looking at the garden to see what else needed to be done, I made a new, comprehensive list.

Use one page of the to-do section for reminders of things you need to do next season. If it's summer, and you think of some chores you'll need to do this fall, make a FALL page and write them down. Doing this has saved me lots of headaches.

Second section: Reference lists.

These are lists that you'll refer back to on occasion.

For example, I'd keep a list of all the yews in the parks system that needed trimmed, a list of all gardens that needed weekly waterings, a list of all places that needed sprayed for bagworms, a list of all the roses that needed to be babied, etc.

I would also keep my running lists in this section, too – lists I keep adding to.

For instance, I kept a list of when different vegetables were ready for harvest – even vegetables I didn't grow, as my friends and relatives reported to me. Then when I made a plan for my veggie garden, I would look at the list to get an idea of when these plants finished up, and then I could figure out when I could take them out and put in a new crop. I also had a list of "seed-to-harvest" times, so I could give each crop enough time to make the harvest date before frost.

You can also keep a wish list – plants and vegetables you'd like to have in your garden.

Third section: Tracking progress.

This is a weekly (or, "whenever it occurs to me to write about it") section as well.

If you plant seeds in a greenhouse, keep track of what seeds you order, when you plant them, when they germinate, how many plants you transplant (and how many survive to maturity), and so forth.

When you finish up in the greenhouse, use these pages to look back and record your thoughts – "I will never again try to start vinca from seeds! Never!! Never!!!" Then you don't annoy yourself by forgetting and buying vinca seeds next year.

You can do the same thing when you move on to the vegetable garden – what dates you tilled the ground, planted the seeds, when they germinated, and so forth. Make notes on yields and how everything tasted. "The yellow crooknecks were definitely not what I'd hoped for. Try yellow zucchini next year."

Be sure to write a vegetable garden overview at season's end, too. "Next year, for goodness' sake, get some 8-foot poles for the beans! Also, drive the poles deeper into the ground so they don't fall over during thunderstorms."

During the winter, you can look back on this section and see ways you can improve your yields and harvest ("The dehydrator worked great on the apples!"), and you can see which of your experiments worked.

Fourth section: Details of the natural world.

When keeping a journal, don't limit yourself to what's going on in your garden. Track events in the natural world, too. Write down when the poplars start shedding cotton or when the Queen's Anne Lace blooms.

You've heard old gardening maxims such as "plant corn when oak leaves are the size of a squirrel's ear," or "prune roses when the forsythia blooms." If the spring has been especially cold and everything's behind, you can rely on nature's cues instead of a calendar when planting or preventing disease outbreaks.

Also, by setting down specific events, you can look at the journal later and say, "Oh, I can expect little caterpillars to attack the indigo plant when the Johnson's Blue geranium is blooming." Then next year, when you notice the buds on your geraniums, you can seek out the caterpillar eggs and squish them before they hatch. An ounce of prevention, see?

When I read back over this section of the journal, patterns start to emerge. I noticed that Stargazer lilies bloom just as the major heat begins. This is no mere coincidence: It's happened for the last three years! So now when I see the large buds, I give the air conditioner a quick checkup.

Fifth section: Notes and comments.

This is more like the journal that most people think of as being a journal – here, you just talk about the garden, mull over how things are looking, or grouse about those supposedly blight-resistant tomatoes that decided to be contrary and keel over from blight.

I generally put a date on each entry, then ramble on about any old thing. You can write a description of the garden at sunset, sketch your peppers, or keep track of the habits of bugs you see crawling around in the plants. This ain't art, this is just fun stuff (which, in the end, yields great dividends).

Maybe you've been to a garden talk on the habits of Asian melons and you need a place to put your notes. Put them here!

This is a good place to put garden plans, too. Years later I run into them again, see old mistakes I've made, and remember neat ideas I haven't tried yet.

Get a calendar.

Then, when December comes, get next year's calendar and the gardening journal and sit down at the kitchen table. Using last year's notes, mark on the calendar events to watch out for -- when the tomatoes first ripen, when the summer heat starts to break, and when you expect certain insects to attack. In the upcoming year, you just look at the calendar and say, "Well, the squash bugs will be hatching soon," so you put on your garden gloves and start smashing the little rafts of red eggs on the plants.

A garden journal can be a fount of information, a source of memories, and most of all, a way to keep organized. Who thought a little spiral notebook could do so much?

If you enjoy this book, grab a copy on Amazon!

Don't Throw in the Trowel in <u>Paperback</u>
Don't Throw in the Trowel on <u>Kindle</u>

Sample for <u>Design of the Times: How to Plan Glorious Landscapes and Gardens</u>

Style: Everybody has it but nobody really knows what it is. And when it comes to garden design, everybody has style. Sometimes, though, they have just haven't figured out what their gardening style is.

Some people lean more toward traditional gardens with flowers to cram them into. Other lean more toward the formal gardens and parterres. Or maybe you might prefer a tropical style with all its orange and yellows and cannas and lush leaves. And some like to mix styles in a fun pastiche of plants and colors.

What do you like? Maybe at this time you don't know. But this book is here to help you find your way and figure it out.

Get the whole family involved with planning your garden!

Rules of (Green) Thumb for Garden Design

Once you have all your garden measured out, sit down with your graph paper, let one square equal one square foot (adjust this if you have the graph paper with the tiny squares), and start putting this all down on paper. Have the top of the paper be north, and draw a little arrow pointing that way to look more official.

As you do, you will find that you'll need to keep running out to measure more things in the yard in order to make everything line up correctly. You've measured the house and driveway, for example, but wait, how many feet do you have between the driveway and the east corner of the house? So you measure that. Where exactly does the oak tree sit in relation to the fence and the house? So you measure that. The fence and the house are not lining up correctly. So you remeasure that and try to figure out if you transposed a measurement. The oak tree seems to have inadvertently shrunk, though you'd measured it twice. Maybe it's time to take up drinking. Well, okay, but only in moderation.

Of course, that's the way the old timers did it. (Note: I am not old.) These days, you can fix up a nice landscape plan on your phone using an app, or get a more elaborate program for your laptop that will do more than just move a tree symbol around until it looks like it's placed right.

Then it's time for the big step: drawing a plan. Measure your garden. To keep your plan simple, let one-half inch equal one foot. Draw the outline of the garden on your paper.

Protip: Once you have this step finished to your satisfaction, take this paper to the copier and make several copies, and use these as the rough drafts of your garden design.

Now play with that outline. Consider the height and width of these plants. Keep short plants in front and tall plants in back, and use those pictures you've clipped (whether out of a magazine or found on the internet) to make sure the colors match. Do you want soft colors, such as purple catmint, pink petunias, and silver Artemisia? Or do you want a fiesta of red salvia and "Yellow Boy" marigolds?

Also, consider when your perennials bloom. You may love purple asters and pink sea thrift, but that color pairing won't be happening, because the asters bloom in fall and the sea thrift blooms in spring.

It's a good idea to put the tall plants in back and short plants in front. Green side up. Match the plants to the amount of sun that's available. Set your shade plants near the trees, while the full sun plants will need to be right out in the sun.

As you draw your plan, generally a good rule of thumb is to arrange them by height – tallest plants in back, shortest ones in the back. Or, as with an island bed, tallest plants in the middle, going to the shortest on the edges. But you can also blend several different varieties of plants that are the same size, the same way as you would blend several different flowers in a flower arrangement, for a good blend of colors and shapes. And you don't have to be exact on regimenting sizes. A garden isn't a lineup of soldiers on dress parade, after all.

You can arrange the plants in any way. You can arrange them in a parterre, a formal setting with neat rows, tidy edged shrubs. Or you can have a wild, natural garden with plants arranged as if they were growing wild. Chances are you will be someplace between these two extremes in your own garden.

Also, to make more of an impact, plant your perennials in drifts of 3, 5, or 7. These groups provide more of an impact than just planting one of every plant (unless you have a specimen plant that's as big as an elephant).

Protip: It's a good idea to have a little out-of-the-way place in your garden where you keep extra plants – those you've picked up when on sale but can't find a place for, plants you've picked up out of curiosity, plants you've gotten from friends and neighbors that don't quite fit into your gardening plan, or things you need to find a proper place for but haven't gotten to yet.

This little garden can get helpful, though. If you have a plant in your regular garden that suddenly croaks, you can grab a full-grown specimen from your little side garden and pop it into your regular garden, if you're so inclined, thereby filling the gap.

You can also keep your cutting garden here, so you can just pop out the back door and cut a few flowers for bouquets inside the house. Then you won't have to swipe flowers from your front gardens and leave holes in it.

Old-timey infomercials were just as bad as today's infomercials.

Always Be On the Lookout for Ideas

Designing a garden is a lot of fun. This is where you get to meet all the possibilities that are open to you. But if you're new to this, coming up with design ideas can be tough. Sometimes that's true of the old gardening pro, too! Here are a few ways to get some good ideas (and these work if you're a seasoned gardener, too).

Visit other gardens to get new ideas for plants and designs, and to see how different combinations work. If you are visiting a botanical garden, keep in mind that some of those plants might not be available to you – but you can certainly get some great ideas about form, color, and good design from these places.

Take pictures or notes of plant combinations you like as you come across them. When I see a landscape design

I like, I make a sketch of it to see how it works, and figure out how I can replicate it at home or elsewhere. Don't be shy about writing down good plant choices, or sketching garden layouts, or taking pictures of gardens with your phone.

Some magazines, books, and websites feature ready-made garden designs. Look over the design, look at the pics, and if you see some plant combination you like, write it down or download the picture. Or pick up the landscape plan for yourself, then modify it to your liking. By playing with ideas, you can come up great garden designs.

Gathering plant ideas.

Sometimes you come up with a great idea for a plant combination that you're dying to try, so you plant the flowers together in the garden – only to find out that one starts blooming two weeks before its partner does, and by the time the second plant starts blooming, the first plant is finished. Don't you just hate that?

If you refer to my chapter about keeping a gardening notebook, I mention keeping running lists for different things going on in your garden as well as events happening in the natural world.

Flip over to your running list section and start a new list: Blooming Times.

Then, all through the year, write down blooming times for every plant that you might want to use in the garden (and even those that you don't).

This is a list you can keep adding to for years and years. What you're doing here is putting down blooming times for any plant you might want to use in the garden, so you can refer back to this later to get flowering combinations that actually work for you in your area – and in your garden.

Protip: Here's a great way to keep really good track of plant colors in your garden. Go into your garden and gather a blossom from the main plants in your design (as well as a colored leaf from any variegated plants or plants with colored leaves.) Then place them all on a color copier or scanner, arrange them carefully on the glass, and make a color copy of them.

As the year passes, as new flowers come into the garden and old ones fade out, repeat this color snapshot. (When you save these pictures, or print them out, be sure to put the date on them, as these color samples will likely be different every year – indeed, every month.) Then, when you go to your local nursery, you can match the bloom times and bloom colors that you have with whatever plants they have in stock.

If you like this book, please leave a review on my Bookbub or Goodreads page. Reviews help me get more readers. Be sure to recommend my books to any of your gardener friends (and even your gardener enemies).

Subscribe to my newsletter
and get a free gardening book:
https://melindacordell.com/subscribe/

melindacordell.com

Me and my worm friends in 2011

ABOUT THE AUTHOR

I've worked in most all aspects of horticulture – garden centers, wholesale greenhouses, as a landscape designer, and finally as city horticulturist, where I took care of 20+ gardens around the city. I live in northwest Missouri with my husband and kids, the best little family that ever walked the earth. In 2012, when I was hugely pregnant, I graduated from Hamline University with a master's of writing for children; three weeks later, I had a son. It was quite a time.

My first book, **Courageous Women of the Civil War: Soldiers, Spies, Medics, and More** was published by Chicago Review Press in August 2016. This is a series of profiles of women who fought or cared for the wounded during the Civil War.

I've been sending novels out to publishers and agents since 1995, and have racked up I don't know how many hundreds of rejections. I kept getting very close – but not close enough. Agents kept saying, "You're a very good writer, you have an excellent grasp of craft, but I just don't feel that 'spark'...." Even after *Courageous Women* was published, they still weren't interested in my books.

In September 2016, I rage-quit traditional publishing and started self-publishing, because I wanted to get my books out to people who *would* feel that 'spark.' In my first year, I published 15 books. This year I plan to repeat that. (When you've been writing novels for over 20 years, you're going to have a bit of a backlog.) I am working my way completely through it and having a complete blast. I love doing cover work and designing the book interiors. I work full-time as a proofreader, so I handle that in my books as well.

And now I'm finding fans of my books who do feel that 'spark.' They're peaches, every one of them.

I'm finally doing what I was put on this earth to do.

There's no better feeling than that.

Thanks so much for reading.